The A to Z of Business Grammar and Style

Copyright © 2015 by Peter Shefston

This version authored by Dr. Peter Shefston

Published by Felden Business Books

All rights reserved. This book or any portion thereof may not be reproduced or used in any manner whatsoever without the express written permission of the publisher except for the use of brief quotations in a book review or scholarly journal.

ISBN 978-1-326-02481-9

First Printing: 2015

2016.25

Contents

Introduction **5**
A to Z **7**
Guidelines for good writing **86**
Writing a business report **88**
email etiquette **90**
Mangled phrases **92**
References **93**

Introduction

Good writing is critical for business, whether you are writing a report or proposal for a customer or communicating with internal colleagues. An important message can easily become lost if it contains grammatical or spelling errors, or it's simply too difficult to read. The rules of grammar and spelling exist for the same reason that rules exist for driving - to avoid accidents and make sure that everyone understands the intentions of others.

This guide has been written with one aim – to improve the quality of written business communications. Some might argue that in a world of text messages and email, grammar and sentence construction become less important; here a few reasons why getting it right is important:

- Often, the only thing we provide to our customers is a written report or document. The quality of our writing is an essential way for them to see the value we add.

- If people cannot understand what you mean, your opportunity to sell or deliver services and products will be wasted. Poor writing suggests a lack of clear thinking.

- You never know how a customer might react to bad writing. While some may be forgiving, others will be frustrated when they see poor use of language and will inevitably think less of you.

Many style guides are available for use by specialists (journalists, legal and medical professionals etc.). This guide has been written specifically to meet the needs of business writers, from those entering business for the first time to experienced people looking for guidance on tricky grammar questions. To use this guide, you do not need to know the difference between a future imperfect and a past participle, or even an adverb from an adjective. By avoiding complex grammatical theory that makes other style guides difficult to read, I hope it's easier to use and that readers will make it an essential reference guide.

Peter Shefston

A to Z

@

Generally known as the 'at sign', its formal name is the 'commercial at'. It is mainly used in email addresses but its use predates computers. Although it is useful shorthand for note taking, in formal writing, do not use it as a substitute for the word *at*.

 The meeting will begin @ four o'clock.

a, an

When placing either *a* or *an* before an abbreviation or acronym, look at whether it's followed by a vowel <u>sound</u>. If it is, use *an*; if not, use *a*. If in doubt say it out loud.

 An HR policy was circulated.

 An FD job has just been advertised.

 A URL for the website.

 A BBC employee.

abbreviations

In a formal report, do not abbreviate words such as *administration (admin.), manager (mgr.), employee (emp'ee), employer (emp'er)* or *approximately (approx.)*.

These abbreviations tend to break the flow and make it harder to understand (especially when writing for an international audience). For the sake of a few keystrokes, avoid lazy abbreviation.

ability, capability, capacity

Ability is a person's mental skill or physical power to do something.

Capability is the general power or ability of a machine or organisation to do something or be used to do something. It can apply to people, but *ability* is usually the simpler choice.

Capacity is the amount that someone or something can get, hold, contain, produce carry or absorb. It describes a person or organisation's physical or mental power to learn something.

about, around

About is preferred to *around* when using numbers.

Use *about* for round numbers, not specific figures.

If a figure is an *estimate*, using the word *about* in the same sentence is redundant. Use one or the other, not both. *About* is not necessary when giving a range – it implies an estimation is being made.

- ✓ There are about 3,000 employees on this site.
- ✗ There are about 10 to 15 interfaces in current use.
- ✗ I estimate there are about 19 offices.

accept, except

Accept means "to receive" or "agree to".

- ✓ Please accept my apology.

Except means "other than" and "to leave out":

- ✓ We agreed on everything except the fee.
- ✓ Send me everything except the appendices.

acronyms

Acronyms are formed from the initial letters of words (whether the result is pronounceable as a word or as a series of letters). Do not use full stops or spaces between initials, including those in proper names. Use all capitals if an abbreviation is pronounced as the individual letters.

  BBC, CEO, US, VAT.

For a full acronym (that is, it can be pronounced as a word) spell it out with an initial capital.

  Nasa, Nato, Unicef

When using an acronym that may be unfamiliar to readers, spell it out in full the first time it is mentioned, followed by the acronym in brackets. The next time it is used, use the acronym alone.

  The decision was made by the Senior Leadership Team (SLT). The SLT meets on a regular basis.

actual, actually

These words should be used to emphasise the truth or facts of a situation, or to stress that something is surprising. However, they are often used as 'filler' or 'crutch' words, so take care, as they can also sound patronising when used to correct someone.

  Despite initial concerns, costs are actually decreasing.

  I'm busy, actually, and I don't have time to help.

addresses

When writing to an external reader, give the full address, including the postcode (postcodes and zipcodes allow people to find buildings more easily online). Formats vary across countries, but in the UK use:

  Our Head Office is located at 123, High Street, Anytown, AB1 2CD.

If a building is very hard to find, consider giving GPS coordinates for anyone using a satellite navigation system.

advance, advanced

If you receive early warning of something or take an action ahead of when it is expected, use *advance*. If something is complex or sophisticated, it is *advanced*.

☑ I received advance warning of the auditor's visit.

☑ We are implementing an advanced finance system.

adverse, averse

Use *adverse* to describe things, conditions or circumstances that are unfavorable, harmful or hostile.

☑ Adverse weather conditions.

Use *averse* to describe a person's feeling of reluctance, distaste or opposition.

☑ The client is highly risk averse.

☒ The client is highly risk adverse.

advice, advise

To *advise* means to tell someone what you think they should do in a particular situation OR to inform someone about a fact or situation in a formal or official way.

☑ I advised her to go home and get some sleep.

☑ Our lawyer will advise the best course of action.

In simple terms, *advice* is what is given.

☑ I was given good advice.

advisor, adviser

Both spellings are correct, with *adviser* being the most common, especially in British English.

affect, effect

Affect (as a verb) means to have an impact on or to change something.

☑ The revised project scope may affect the delivery date.

Effect means the result or outcome of something.

☑ What effect will this have on the problem?

agree to, agree with, agree on

Use *agree to* when expressing consent to do something.

☑ He agreed to pay for the additional time needed.

Use *agree with* to express similar opinions on or about something.

☑ He agreed with his manager about the appraisal.

Use *agree on* when writing about the subject of the agreement.

☑ They agreed on the need to defer payment.

all ready, already

Use *all ready* to say someone is prepared to do something.
Use *already* to say something happened earlier.

☑ The contractor is all ready to begin work; in fact, he's already started.

allude, elude

Allude means to suggest or call attention to indirectly or hint at.

☑ I will allude briefly to the main points.

Elude means "to escape capture" or "to escape notice or understanding".

☑ The solution to this problem eludes me.

If something eludes you it is *elusive*, not *illusive*

allusion, illusion

An *allusion* is a passing or casual reference to something. An *illusion* is a trick or mirage.

alternative, alternate

An alternative is a choice between two courses of action; there can never be more than one main action and one alternative. If there are more than two, *option* or *choice* is preferred.

☑ We need to find an alternative solution.

☒ Several alternatives are available.

☑ We need to find other options.

The word alternate (pronounced 'alter-nate') can mean the same as alternative, but it is mostly used in American English - it is rarely used in British English.

When pronounced as 'ol-tur-nut', this word can mean 'every other'.

☑ The board meets on alternate Wednesdays.

altogether, all together

Altogether means "completely, or the whole amount or number of something".

- ✓ The office will be closed down altogether. *(Completely or fully is better.)*

All together describes everything or everyone together at once or in one place.

- ✓ We were all together for the meeting.

ampersand (&)

An ampersand symbol (&) should not be used in formal writing as a substitute for the word 'and'. Its use should be limited to the following:

- ✓ Company names e.g. Bill & Ben Consulting.
- ✓ Academic references e.g. (Smith & Jones, 2010).
- ✓ Accepted paired words, such as Learning & Development.
- ✗ Tom & I will be at the meeting.

American or British English?

When writing for an exclusively North American audience, American spelling and grammar should be used. For a mixed or European audience, or where the main recipient is based in Europe, British English should be the standard. In this case, the following words should take British English spellings:

- ✓ Analyse/analysis; organise/organisation; realise/realisation; finalise (use of 's' rather than 'z').
- ✓ Centre; theatre ('...re' rather than '...er').
- ✓ Colour; labour; flavour ('...our' rather than '...or').
- ✓ Programme (not program, except when it refers to a computer program).

Some British readers are easily irritated by American spelling, so while you may be very relaxed about it, consider that your reader may not be.

among, amongst, between

Among is used to describe something that is a member of a larger set.

☑ Birmingham was among the main locations being considered.

Amongst is a variant of *among* and means the same thing. *Amongst* is used in British, Australian, and Canadian English, but it is rare in American English and may sound pompous or archaic (see also *while/whilst*).

Between is not limited to two parties and should be used to describe a relationship.

☑ Common processes exist between the three factories.

and, but

It's generally believed that a sentence should never begin with *and* or *but*. But this is a myth – they are simple, clear and correct transition words between related (*and*) and contrasting (*but*) sentences. Use it for emphasis or drama, but don't overdo it as the impact may be lost.

A comma is not necessary following *and* or *but* at the beginning of a sentence.

anymore, any more

Anymore refers to time, typically in a negative sense. It means "no longer" or "from now on" and tends to be used in American English rather than British English.

☑ Alice doesn't live here anymore.

Any more refers to number or quantity, meaning "any additional", "no further" or "no more" and is used mostly in a negative sense. Here's an example using both terms in a single sentence:

☑ I don't buy stationery anymore - I don't need any more stationery.

anytime, any time

Anytime means at some point in time.

☑ The system could fail anytime soon.

Any time refers to a quantity of time.

☑ I don't have any time to do this.

anyway, any way

Anyway means "even so" or "however" and tends to be used in spoken form only.

☑ "Anyway, what shall we do next?"

Any way refers to the possibility of something.

☑ There isn't any way that this could be made to work (clumsy).

☑ There is no way this could be made to work (less clumsy).

☑ Is there any way this could be made to work?

apostrophe

An apostrophe denotes a connection between two things.

☑ The company's profit (meaning the profit of the company).

Correct placement of the apostrophe is important – this is usually determined by whether the subject is singular or plural.

☑ The employee's manager (meaning the manager of one employee).

The employees' manager (meaning the manager of more than one employee).

A common mistake is to use an apostrophe to make a word plural. Apostrophes **never** make a word plural – this is often known as a 'grocer's apostrophe' or a 'yob's apostrophe'.

 Consultants, laptops, payrolls

 Consultant's, laptop's, payroll's

exceptions
In very rare cases, words can look odd in their plural form without an apostrophe, for example:

Dot the is and cross the ts.

In these cases, it is acceptable to use an apostrophe.

 Dot the 'i's and cross the 't's.

 The company scored A's in its evaluation report.

plurals
There is often confusion when using apostrophes for plurals. Follow these rules:

Add an apostrophe to plural nouns ending in 's'

 The girls' books (the books of more than one girl).

For singular nouns ending in 's', do not add an 's' after the apostrophe:

 The bus' seats.

If the sentence looks complicated or you are unsure, rephrase the possessive relationship as an 'of' phrase

 The employees of the manager.

place names
Some place names and street names have an apostrophe and some don't – this can't be predicted and must be checked.

☑ Times Square.

☑ Land's End.

time
Use apostrophes with phrases denoting periods of time. Use an apostrophe if you can replace the apostrophe with 'of'.

☑ You must give one month's notice (single form).

☑ You must give three months' notice (plural form).

Do not use an apostrophe to form plurals of decades.

☑ The system has been in place since the early 1990s.

☒ The system has been in place since the early 1990's.

around, round

Around has several meanings, including located or situated on every side, facing in the opposite direction and in the vicinity. Around is slightly more formal.

☑ We were driving around aimlessly all weekend.

Round is a more concerned with direction or shape.

☑ I took a tour round the factory.

See also *about*.

as per

This means 'in accordance with'.

   As per your instructions.

However, this phrase is generally considered stuffy and archaic and should be avoided.

assure, ensure, insure

To *assure* a person of something is to make him or her confident of it.
To *ensure* that something happens is to make certain that it does.

To *insure* is to issue an insurance policy.

basically

This word is unnecessary, basically.

barter, haggle

When you exchange or trade something you have for another item or service, you *barter*.

When you offer to buy something for less money than the vendor is asking you are engaged in *haggling* or *bargaining*, not bartering.

 I plan to haggle over the price.

 I plan to barter over the price.

bear, bare

Bear refers to bearing a load or weight and is sometimes used as a metaphor.

 Please bear with me at this difficult time.

Bare means naked.

 Please bare with me (this implies you want to get naked with someone).

Likewise, the same rule applies to *bearing* (as in 'bearing in mind' or load bearing') and *baring (*as in baring one's soul*)*.

See also *homophones*.

beside, besides

Beside means 'next to', 'at the side of' or 'by'. Avoid *besides*.

☑ 'Where is the new office? It's right beside the main road. You can't miss it!'

It is also used in the expression *beside the point* when referring to something that is not relevant to the subject being discussed.

☑ He mentioned the lack of office space, but that's beside the point.

Besides means 'in addition to', 'furthermore', 'as well as' or 'apart from'.

☑ "Which departments have you worked in besides finance and procurement?"

☑ The project has run out of funding. Besides, everyone seems to have lost interest in it.

better, best

Better is used when comparing two things; *best* is used when comparing three or more things.

☑ Which is the better of these two cars?

☑ Which is the best car in the car park?

The same principle applies to greater/greatest; smaller/smallest; bigger/biggest; older/oldest; worse/worst and so on.

biennial, biannual

Biennial means lasting for two years or occurring every two years. *Biannual* means occurring twice a year.

To avoid confusion, it is preferable to avoid these words, since their intent is unclear. Use 'every two years' or 'twice a year'.

biweekly

The use of *biweekly* (or *bi-weekly*) is even less clear than biennial/biannual. American English tends to mean every two weeks, but British English favours an interpretation based on twice a week. It is best avoided, simply state either every two weeks or twice a week.

books/films/songs/games etc.

Capitalise the first word of the title, and all words within the title except articles (a/an/the), prepositions (to/on/for etc.) and conjunctions (but/and/or etc.).

 Always Look on the Bright Side of Life.

 Always Look On The Bright Side Of Life.

borrow, lend

Lend - to give to someone else to use for a period of time.

Borrow - to receive from someone else for a period of time

 You may borrow my book, which I am happy to lend to you.

brackets (parentheses, like these)

Use brackets to add extra information, such as a translation, dates, an explanation or a definition.

 The company (which employs two thousand people) wishes to relocate to another city.

There should be no space between the bracket and the start of the first word, or before the closing bracket.

 The company (which employs two thousand people) wishes to relocate to another city.

brackets [square, like these]

Use brackets to enclose comments, corrections, references or translations made by a subsequent author or editor or to describe non-verbal activities.

 The Finance Director related an anecdote about a recent workplace incident [Laughter].

brackets - punctuation

Include full stops/exclamation marks/question marks/quotation marks **inside** a bracket if the complete sentence/quote is within the brackets; otherwise, punctuate outside the bracket.

 December payroll runs on the 18th (this is earlier than usual).

 December payroll runs on the 18th. (This is earlier than usual.)

branding

Companies invest heavily in corporate branding and it's essential that the most up to date version of logos and document styles is used.

Consult your company intranet to find the latest templates and styles.

bring, take

Americans in particular tend to get this distinction wrong. The correct usage generally depends on your point of reference for the action. The rule is: you ask people to bring things to the place you are, and you take things to the place you are going.

You bring things here and take things there.

 Could you please bring the file to the meeting?

 I need to take work home with me. (Said while you are at work.)

bullet points

Lists and bullet points are useful in text to save space and improve readability (see also *lists*). Here are some guidelines for using bullets, numbers or other punctuation marks in a vertical list:

- End the introduction to the list with a colon (:) as in the sentence before this point.
- Use a full stop (period) after each point if one or more of the items are complete sentences. Do not mix sentences and non-sentences in a list.
- Capitalise the first word in each item if one or more of the items are complete sentences. Preferably, all or none of the items should be a complete sentence.
- Don't end bullet point list items with a semicolon.
- Use bullets before each item in the list when rank or sequence is not important. If order is important, use numbers or letters.
- Use a consistent style of bullet point throughout – do not mix square, round, hyphens etc.
- Avoid multiple layers of bullet points – if you must, use different bullet styles at each level.
- Consider a 6 point spacing after each bullet as this helps the reader (as in this list).

capitalisation

There is a tendency in much modern writing to insert capital letters randomly into text. Avoid RACs (Random Acts of Capitalisation) - do not use a capital letter unless it is absolutely required.

 The report will need to be approved by your manager.

 The Report will need to be approved by your Manager.

Note that certain legal contracts require specific words to be capitalised (for example, *the Customer*) that would not be required in normal grammar.

cite, site, sight

You *cite* an author in a footnote, endnote or reference section.

The *site* of something is where it is taking place.

You go *sight*seeing when on holiday.

classic, classical

Classic refers to something that is an outstanding example of its kind, such as a classic car.

Classical refers to periods of time such as ancient Greece or Rome or to well-defined historical periods of culture and science. It also refers to European orchestral music of the late 18th and early 19th centuries.

clause

A clause is the smallest grammatical unit that can express a complete idea. An awareness of clauses can improve your business writing considerably.

An *independent clause* expresses a complete thought. Sentences look odd when you try to put two independent clauses together, often joined using a comma, in what is called a 'comma splice'.

 A clause is the smallest grammatical unit that can express a complete idea, an awareness of clauses can considerably improve your business writing.

In this example, the reader is being given too much information at once and the poor comma can't cope with it. The cure is to insert a more robust form of punctuation such as a full stop (period), semicolon, or possibly a joining word.

 A clause is the smallest grammatical unit that can express a complete idea; an awareness of clauses can considerably improve your business writing.

 A clause is the smallest grammatical unit that can express a complete idea and an awareness of clauses can considerably improve your business writing.

Do not use a comma, or phrases such as 'nevertheless', 'therefore', 'however' etc. to join two main clauses.

 The business processes were effective, demonstrated by the low cost of operation.

 The business processes were effective, therefore management was pleased with the results

See also *clauses*.

A *dependent or subordinate clause* is usually the supporting part of a sentence, and it cannot stand by itself as a meaningful proposition (idea).

 Because we need to make progress with the project.

The cure is to insert a comma and add more information.

Because we need to make progress with the project, we will need considerably more money.

coarse, course

Coarse means rough, crude, of low quality or not fine in texture.

Course has many meanings, including education delivered in a series of lessons (training course); a direction (the course of a river); a series of events (a course of action); part of a meal (main course); an area of land (or water) for sport (golf course); naturally (of course).

See also *homophones*.

collaborate, corroborate

People who work together on a project are said to *collaborate*.

When someone supports your opinion or testimony, they *corroborate*.

colon

A colon is used to introduce a sub clause or list which follows logically from the text before it. It should only be used after a clause (part of a sentence) that could stand alone and makes complete sense on its own.

The first part of the text sets up the idea and the words after the colon deliver the content. It's the equivalent of saying "I'm going to tell you something now…here it comes: this is it".

 The company will be investing in a number of opportunities: property, shares and oil.

 The manager was afraid of one thing: failure.

Do not use a colon if the two parts of the sentence are not logically connected.

 The payroll did not run yesterday: the staff restaurant will be closed on Friday.

A colon should be followed by a single space with no space before it and no dash after it. Opinion is mixed about following a colon with a capital letter, but in general, do not use a capital letter unless the first word is a proper noun or what follows forms a complete sentence.

comma

A comma is the equivalent of taking a short breath and helps to slow down the reader and take in the information given, like a grammatical speed bump. It also clarifies meaning by breaking up a phrase - consider these very different sentences:

Let's eat, father.
Let's eat father.

Use a pair of commas to surround a clause. A clause adds descriptive information – you can tell it's a clause if it can be removed without losing the meaning of the sentence. Only '*which*' or '*who*' can be used in this type of clause.

☑ The finance director, who had been employed for forty years, was planning to retire soon.

☑ The payroll system, which was now five years old, was increasingly inefficient.

In a list, there is no comma between the penultimate item and '*and*'/'*or*':

☒ He can speak French, Spanish, and German.

☑ I can offer you Monday, Tuesday or Wednesday to meet.

One exception to this is where a comma prevents ambiguity – this is sometimes referred to as the 'Oxford comma', for example where the word 'and' is used elsewhere in the sentence.

☑ Our key priorities are performance management, learning and development, and talent management.

A comma should be followed by a single space.

company names

In general, use the same spelling, capitalisation and style that companies use themselves, even if it is not grammatically correct.

✓ easyJet, eBay, ebookers, serco

Companies as legal entities are always singular so use *is, was, it* and singular forms of verbs when referring to them.

✓ OurCo is likely to bid on this contract.

✗ OurCo are pleased to respond to this RFI.

See also *singular, plural, department names*.

compare to, compare with

Both are correct but each has a different meaning.

Compare to suggests similarities (where the similarity is the key point).

✓ A Mercedes can be compared to a BMW – they are both German luxury cars.

Compare with points out differences between things (where the difference is the key point).

✓ CEOs make 331 times as much as their employees, compared with 42 times in the 1980s.

complement, compliment

Complement means to make complete or give a mutual benefit.

✓ The two technologies will complement each other.

Compliment means to praise or reward:

✓ He received a compliment from the client.

✓ A complimentary copy is provided free of charge.

See also *homophones*.

comprising, comprises, comprised

Although in common usage, *comprising of*, *comprises of* and *comprised of* are incorrect. 'The 'of' part is not necessary.

✓ The advisory board comprises six members.

✗ The advisory board is comprised of six members.

continual, continuous

Continual things come and go. If you have continual arguments with your colleague, it means they stop sometimes. The same applies to *continually*.

✓ My car breaks down continually.

Continuous and *continuously* means something never stops.

✓ There is a continuous rattling noise coming from my car engine.

contractions

Contractions are formed by omitting letters from the middle of a word. They are formed by dropping a letter and inserting an apostrophe.

Cannot	▶ Can't
Could not	▶ Couldn't
Has not	▶ Hasn't
Do not	▶ Don't
He will	▶ He'll
Will not	▶ Won't
They are	▶ They're (do not confuse with their or there)

Do not overuse contractions - they can be irritating and distracting, potentially making a serious report sound frivolous. However, contractions can help lighten the tone of a document and make it sound less formal and bureaucratic. Try to strike a balance.

Do not use an apostrophe before contractions that are generally accepted as words in their own right.

- ✓ He's on the *phone*.
- ✓ He had swine *flu*.
- ✗ There's no vaccine for all types of 'flu.

could have/could of

Frankly, anyone saying or writing '*could of*' should be fired on the spot. It's just wrong.

currencies

When referring to a currency, if the whole word is used, it is lower case: euro, pound, sterling etc.

Abbreviate dollars like this:

- ✓ $50 (US dollars).
- ✓ A$50 (Australian dollars).

customers

Do not refer to customers as 'they' or 'their' or 'third party'. These words can sound cold, distant and bureaucratic, and possibly a little rude. In the eyes of the reader, the customer is not 'they', but 'we'.

It is much better to refer to a customer by name.

- ✓ PharmaCo will need to replace the finance system in the next two years.
- ✗ They will need to replace their finance system in the next two years.

dashes

A single dash can add a touch of drama – like this. A pair of dashes is an alternative to commas or brackets when you want to draw the reader's attention to something surprising or unusual.

 The company – which has been investigating this problem for some time – is now ready to progress with the solution.

Do not overly use dashes – like in this example – that contains far too many dashes – and can irritate the reader. Commas, brackets and semicolons are usually better in moderation.

data

Data is a plural word, with datum as the singular. Therefore, the correct use is 'data are…' which looks odd but is correct.

 All the data are correct.

dates

The US, UK and Europe use different formats for dates.

simplified form
7/12/15 to an American is July 12, 2015.
7/12/15 to a British person is 7 December, 2015.

In some parts of Northern Europe a descending format is used: 15/7/12 is 2015 / July / 12.

Because of the many different formats in use, it is important to avoid ambiguity. When writing for a mixed audience, write the date out in full.

using dates in formal (letters)
Americans would write October 30, 2015 at the top of the page before the recipient's address, top left. Britons would write 30 October, 2015 after the recipient's address, usually on the right.

In either case, the modern form is not to use 'th' etc. with dates – just the number and month.

- ✓ Easter this year is on 13 April.
- ✗ 11th November is Armistice Day.

Use days with dates only for emphasis or the avoidance of confusion or ambiguity.

spans of numbers and years
Simplify periods of time where it is not ambiguous to do so.

- ✓ The system was implemented between 2007-09.

If using 'from' with a start date or time, always use *to* to indicate the end date or time rather than a dash; alternatively, just use a dash without the 'from'.

- ✓ The holiday year runs from January to December.
- ✓ The holiday year runs January-December.
- ✗ The holiday year runs from January–December.

department names
Capitalise department names <u>only</u> when the word is used as part of the title of a department, but not when referring to a function or idea in general.

- ✓ The Legal Department provides a service to the global business.
- ✗ This is a Legal issue.

In general, department names are always singular. However, you should use the singular when referring to the group as a whole unit and the plural form when the focus is on the group as a collection of individuals.

 The Finance Department is on the second floor

 The Finance Department are unhappy with their pay

See also *singular, plurals*.

dependant, dependent

A *dependant* is a person who relies on another, especially a family member, for financial support.

☑ He is a single man with no dependants.

Dependent means contingent on or determined by:

☑ The decision is dependent on a number of complex factors.

In American English, *dependent* can be used for both meanings. Saying *depending on* or *depends on* may be less clumsy.

different from, different to

Different from is traditionally the correct form, although *different to* is widely accepted.

Different than is frowned on in British English.

It is always 'differs from', not 'differs to'.

diffuse, defuse

Diffuse means to spread out over a wide area or between a large number of people.

Defuse means (literally) to remove the fuse from a bomb or metaphorically to reduce the tension in a situation.

See also *homophones*.

discreet, discrete

Discreet means to show discernment or judgement in speech and action; to be judicious, prudent, circumspect, cautious.

☑ Make sure you are discreet when sharing salary information.

Discrete means separate, detached from others or individually distinct.

☑ A room is a discrete space within a house.

disinterested, uninterested

Disinterested means impartial, unbiased, neutral, not having a stake in the outcome.

An *uninterested* person is bored, unconcerned or indifferent.

E

each other, one another

Use *each other* where there are only two people.

☑ The HR Director and Finance Manager shared holiday calendars with each other.

Use *one another* if it refers to more than two people.

☑ The entire HR team shares holiday dates with one another.

economic, economical

Economic refers to the science of economics or the economy.

Economical means good value or return in relation to the resources used or money spent, or sparing in the use of resources or money.

☑ This car is very economical.

☒ He is economic with the truth.

effect, affect

See *affect, effect*

eldest, oldest

These two words are essentially the same.

☑ Bill is the oldest member of the team.

☑ Bill is the eldest member of the team.

Eldest can only refer to a person, whereas *oldest* can also include things.

Eldest (and elder) generally refer to relative age within a family, team or group (you cannot say the eldest of the cars).

For the usage of elder/eldest and older/oldest, see better/best.

email addresses

These are case sensitive in the part before the @: *Company@admin* is not the same as *company@admin*. In practice, the majority of ISPs ignore this distinction, but consider carefully whether to use upper case.

The word '*email*' does not require either capitalisation or a hyphen.

en route

Not *on route,* although this is the direct translation from the French expression. If you are going to borrow a foreign term, you should make sure it is used authentically. Otherwise, say *on the way.*

enquiry/inquiry

Enquiry is used for general senses of 'ask'.

Inquire and *inquiry* are more typically used in US English and *enquire* and *enquiry* are mostly used in British English. In the UK, *inquiry* is reserved for a formal investigation.

etc.

Etc. is a shortened form of the Latin expression et cetera, meaning "and other things", or "and so forth". Use *etc.* when suggesting there are other similar, well known items in a list. Do not mix 'such as' and 'etc.' in the same statement.

Some modern formats suggest that no full stop (period) is required, but this usage is not well developed and may upset some readers (and spell checkers).

e.g.

e.g. (*exempli gratia*) – means 'such as' or 'for example'; use with examples which are not complete (in lower case and do not follow it with a comma).

If you are using Latin abbreviations, make sure you know what they mean and when to use them. A modern trend is to NOT use full stops (written as eg) - this is acceptable as long as you are consistent.

✓ Many brands of car are available, e.g. Ford, BMW, Audi, Honda, Toyota.

Do not use e.g. if the list is complete:

✗ There are seven colours in a rainbow e.g. red, orange, yellow, green, blue, indigo, violet.

ellipsis

An ellipsis (a string of full stops) is normally used to add drama and tension to a sentence. It can either be a delay before the next sentence or at the end of a sentence. Its place in sentences influences whether a capital letter follows an ellipsis.

✓ Behind him stood a figure......it was ghostly grey.

elude, allude

See *allude, elude*.

embed, imbed

Embed means 'to fix (an object) firmly and deeply in a surrounding mass'.

Although *imbed* is the oldest variation of this word, *embed* is the more common modern use.

every day/everyday

Every day is used to describe something that happens daily.

✓ It happens every day.

✗ It happens everyday.

Everyday is an adjective meaning 'commonplace' or 'all the time'.

✓ An everyday mistake.

farther, further

Farther and *further* are used to describe distance. There is no difference in meaning between them, although *further* is more common.

☑ We can't go any further; the road's blocked.

☑ How much farther are we going?

Farther is more commonly used to refer to distance away from the speaker.

☑ He could see a small boat on the farther shore.

fewer v less

Less is used when referring to things which are not countable objects. If you could use *much* to describe having a lot of something, use *less*. *Fewer* is used with countable objects. If you could use *many* to describe having a lot of the noun, use *less*.

☑ 'I can't eat that much cheese: please give me less.'

☑ 'I can't eat that many carrots, please give me fewer.'

focused, focussed

Focus means 'the centre of interest or activity'.

The American spelling is usually *focused,* while in Britain, the spelling is often *focussed*. Both are correct, as are other derivatives such as *focusing/focussing*. Whatever you choose, make sure you are consistent.

forward, forwards

Forwards generally relates to a physical move or direction.

☑ He drove the car forwards.

Forward typically refers to time.

☑ The meeting was brought forward to 2pm.

Take care when using the word in reference to time; "moving a meeting forward" could be interpreted to mean earlier in time (closer to you) or later (further away). The same problem arises when discussing moving a meeting back – to some people this means earlier, for others it means later.

The expression *going forward(s)* should be avoided (see *clichés*) – use *in future* instead.

foreword

A *foreword* is found at the beginning of a book, usually written by the author to provide an overview or commentary, literally a 'fore word', but it's one word.

full stop, exclamation mark and question mark

Use a full stop, exclamation mark or question mark (but only one) at the end of every sentence. The excessive use of question marks in written communications (especially emails) can be perceived as anger.

☑ What time did you leave last night?

☑ Go home now!

Use a full stop, not a question mark, at the end of a reported question.

☑ He asked if I wanted to go home that morning.

Only use a question mark for a direct question (whether in quotation marks or not).

'Do you want to go home this morning?' he asked.

   He asked if I wanted to go home?

Use a full stop, not an exclamation mark, at the end of a reported imperative.

   He asked me to wait for him.

goal, objective

A *goal* tends to be more general in nature, sometimes without specific tactics.

Objectives are all about tactics or action plans to get from where you are to where you want to be.

A *goal* defines the direction and destination, but the road to get there is accomplished by a series of *objectives*.

gone, went

Went is the PAST TENSE of the verb 'to go' and needs no other verbs to support it.

 I went to the customer's office.

Gone is the PAST PARTICIPLE (i.e. a completed action) of the verb 'to go' and needs another verb to help it along such as has, had and have.

 My manager has gone out for the day.

See also *verbs*.

haggle, barter

See *barter, haggle*

hereby

Hereby is a very formal word, mostly used by lawyers and priests. It can sound archaic in modern business communications.

herewith

An archaic word that sounds very formal and bureaucratic. In a physical document, say *enclosed*; for an email say *attached*.

historic, historical

Historic means something important or influential in history.

 The signing of the Magna Carta was a historic point in English history.

Historical refers to anything from the past, important or not.

 Those files contain historical records of insurance claims.

holidays

See months, days and holidays.

homophones

A *homophone* is a word that sounds the same as another word but differs in spelling. For this reason, homophones are a major source of spelling errors in business writing. The following are examples:

- compliment/ complement
- stationary/stationery
- their/they're/there
- whose/who's
- your/you're

There are too many to provide an exhaustive list, although some of the most common words are mentioned throughout this book. It's important to check the spelling whenever you encounter a word that falls into this category.

however

When using *however* to mean "nevertheless", always follow it with a comma.

☑ However, there is a better solution.

Consider pausing early in the sentence and inserting *however* between commas.

☑ The payroll function, however, reports directly to the Chief Finance Officer.

However also means 'despite' and does not require a comma:

☑ However hard he tried, he could not succeed.

Avoid using *however* to join independent clauses (see also *clauses*).

hyphens

Hyphens help provide clarity by linking certain words together. Consider the difference between these two sentences:

Employees will work twenty four-hour shifts
Employees will work twenty-four hour shifts

Use hyphens in a phrase before a noun:

☑ An up-to-date list.

Before a proper name, number or date:

☑ Pre-2000 cars.

Hyphens can be used to join ordinarily separate words into single words:

☑ XML documents must be well-formed texts.

Do not use a hyphen to make a new word if it is already a recognised word:

☑ Send me an email when you're ready to proceed.

Do not use a hyphen before a noun where the first element ends in *-ly* (but any other adverbs do take a hyphen):

☒ She was a highly-respected manager.

I/me

The incorrect usage of *I* and *me* is a common error. Ironically, it's a mistake often made through a desire to speak and write properly. The rule is quite simple – when constructing a sentence, first remove the other person, form it properly, then add the other person back in.

Tip: *I* usually appears at the start of a sentence, *me* usually appears at the end.

 Bob and I will join you at lunchtime.

 Bob and me will join you at lunchtime. (You wouldn't say *me will join you at lunchtime!*)

 Send the documents to Bob and me.

 Send the documents to Bob and I. (You wouldn't say *send the documents to I.*)

i.e.

i.e. [*id est*] – means *that is*; use it with definitions or lists which are complete (in lower case and do not follow it with a comma).

 Replies should be received by close of business on Friday (i.e. 5pm).

idioms

An idiom is a combination of words that have a figurative meaning, are generally understood by native speakers and in common use. Take care when writing for an international audience as your intended meaning may be lost.

You should keep an eye out for the report.

  I am just pulling your leg.

See *slang, metaphors*

if, whether

If is used to ask an indirect yes-no question. *If* is more common than *whether*.

✓ I asked if I could take the day off.

Whether is preferred in more formal contexts:

✓ The manager asked whether the candidate should be hired.

infer, imply

Infer is to make an assumption about a statement which has not been explicitly stated, to 'read between the lines'.

Imply is to suggest something without explicitly stating it: to hint at something (usually something negative).

✓ He said that there was a problem with the project. I inferred that he thought this was my fault and resented what he was implying.

inquiry, enquiry

See *enquiry, inquiry*

it's, its

It's is a contraction of it is.

Its is the possessive form (concerned with belonging) and does not require an apostrophe.

  The cat has been out in the rain and its paws are muddy.

  The cat has been out in the rain and it's paws are muddy.

Similar words are *yours, ours, hers, theirs whose*.

job titles

Opinions are mixed on this topic but the general consensus is that job titles should be lower case *unless* the job title forms an acronym. However, where a job title follows a person's name, the title should be capitalised.

☑ Bill Smith, Marketing Director.

☑ Please refer this to the finance director.

☑ It requires approval by the CEO.

journal articles

When referring to a published article, only capitalise the first word (and any proper nouns).

☑ He has published an article called 'Developing a business case for investment'.

justification of text

Justified text is where text is aligned along both the left and right margins, as in this book. An alternative is 'ragged right' where text does not go to the right hand margin but wraps around whenever a word is too long to fit that line.

To some extent, the use of justification is about personal preference, although there are pros and cons of each. Justification sometimes leads to typographic anomalies, for example, extremely large spaces may appear between words on lines with only two or three words.

It's more important that a document consistently uses the same style of justification throughout.

kind regards

This phrase is often placed at the end of an email and is probably derived from the more formal phrase *kindest regards*. When studied, the phrase seems to be meaningless - it means 'I'm sending you a greeting in a kind way'. It may not be appropriate for all communications, so use carefully.

lead, led

When referring to something in the past, the correct word is *led*. The word *lead* cannot be used as a substitute for *led* (the confusion possibly comes from the way that the past form of *read* rhymes with *red*).

 Tomorrow I will lead the meeting.

☑ Yesterday, I led the meeting.

(Led Zeppelin fans will be aware of the history of that spelling.)

lend, borrow

See *borrow, lend*

learned, learnt

Learnt is more common in British English, and *learned* in American English. The use of *learnt* is considered a spelling error by many Americans, but both are acceptable in the UK.

See also *spelled* and *spelt*.

less v fewer

See *fewer v less*

licence, license

In UK English, *licence* is a noun:

 I have a licence to drive my car.

In the US, the normal form is *license*. In both the UK and US, the verb form is license.

 We plan to license our financial advisers.

lists

Lists are useful in text to save space and improve readability. Apply the following guidelines:

- Put words and ideas common to all items in the introductory sentence.
- List only comparable items; choose list items that form a logical group.
- Present only one idea in each item.
- Use only words, phrases or short sentences.
- Explain what the list is about before you give it.
- Do not overuse lists or make them too long.
- Use consistent punctuation and capitalisation in list items.

When listing information in paragraph form, use commas to separate items in the list if the items are brief and have little or no internal punctuation. If the items are complex, separate them with semicolons. Use a colon to introduce a list only if a full sentence or clause comes before it. The introductory statement should end with *the following, as follows* or a similar phrase.

 You should expect your vendor to do the following: offer regular maintenance, train end users and respond quickly to service requests.

Or simply use an introductory sentence followed by a colon:

 I think you should: (1) improve your business skills, (2) get more product knowledge and (3) increase your productivity.

See also 'bullet points'

literally

Literally means just that – the words that are used are exactly true, without exaggeration.

✓ We have received literally thousands of complaints.

Although some modern linguists suggest that it is acceptable to use *literally* as hyperbole for dramatic effect, in business writing this could be misleading.

✗ There is literally no way to recover from this error.

lose, loose

Lose is a verb

✓ We must not lose this contract.

Loose is a word meaning free from anything that binds or restrains, uncombined or not bound together

✓ The papers were loose in the folder.

✗ We must not loose this contract.

lie, lay

Lie means to recline or rest on a surface.

✓ I want to lie down and rest.

Lay means to put or place something somewhere

✓ Lay the book on the shelf

login, log-in, log in

Login, spelled as one word (or more formally, *log-in*), is a noun that refers to the process of accessing a system. *Log-in* is generally used in preference to *log-on*.

☑ Enter your login details to access your email.

☑ Enter your log-in details to access your email.

Log in is two words when it functions as a verb.

☑ To access your email, log in with your user name and password.

maybe, may be

Maybe is an adverb that can be substituted with *perhaps* or *possibly*.

 Maybe we will have a weekend away.

May be means *might be* or *could be:*

 It may be that more funding is required for this project.

methodology, method

Methods are the tools, techniques or processes that are used to conduct research or run a project, including surveys, interviews or participant observation. Methods and how they are used are shaped by *methodology*.

Methodology is about the principles that guide research practices or overall approach to a project. *Methodology* explains why we're using certain methods or tools.

metaphors

Metaphors can add colour and richness to your writing. However, sporting metaphors do not travel well – describing someone's behaviour as 'offside' or stating 'we're in the ninth inning' may confuse.

See also *idioms, slang*.

months, days and holidays
Months, days and holidays should be capitalised.

☑ The project starts in November.

☑ The project starts after Christmas.

miss, mrs., ms
Follow a woman's preference in being addressed as Miss, Mrs, or Ms. If you are unsure of a woman's preference, use Ms. The term 'Mx' Is increasingly appearing as a gender neutral title.

my, myself
The use of myself, yourself, yourselves and himself has grown in recent years. In most cases, it is incorrect and 'me', 'you' or 'him' are most often the right word to use.

☑ Please contact me with any questions.

☒ Please contact myself with any questions.

You would never say:

☒ "Myself will meet you tomorrow"

So you would also not say:

☒ "Bill and myself will meet you tomorrow"

The correct use is:

☑ Bill and I will meet you tomorrow.

You can use the word *myself* when "you" are doing something to "you" (where the word *myself* is called a reflexive pronoun).

☑ I asked myself a question.

☑ I did it myself.

Another case where it is correct to use *myself* is when you are both the subject and the object of a sentence. For example, "I see myself as the next CEO" or, "I'm going to treat myself to a day off."

In both of these cases you are the object of your own action, so *myself* is the right word to use.

See also *you, yourself.*

names and titles

Give people's title, forename and surname when they are first mentioned. On subsequent mentions, use either their surname only or title and surname (unless further information is required to prevent ambiguity), but be consistent.

 Dr John Smith was present at the ceremony, as was Professor Susan Jones. Dr Smith had to leave early.

 Dr John Smith and Professor Susan.

people's initials
Use a space to separate each initial, not full stops (periods)

 J R R Tolkien.

 J.R.R. Tolkien.

nett, net

As well as being something for catching fish and an abbreviation for the (inter)net, *net* also refers to the result of a calculation, such as the amount left from gross pay after taxes and deductions (i.e. net pay).

Nett is an older British version of the same word, now rarely used except when referring to weights.

next, this, last

Take care when referring to future events using next, this or last.

For example, if today is Wednesday, when referring to 'next Friday', some people may mean this coming Friday (Friday of this week) or the Friday after that (Friday of the next week). People differ in how they use these words, so it is always best to clarify to avoid ambiguity.

The same is true when using *last* – saying "I met the customer last Monday" may mean the most recent Monday, or the Monday of last week.

none, non

None is a noun meaning 'not any'.

 None of the managers are available today.

Non is typically a prefix that negates what follows and is usually followed by a hyphen.

 This is a non-smoking area.

 Non of the managers are available today.

numbers (small)

Spell out whole number words for one to ten; use figures for numbers above ten.

 The company runs four monthly payrolls and two weekly payrolls.

 The company employs 32 people in the HR service centre.

If there are a lot of figures in a paragraph or text, with some above ten and some below, use figures throughout to allow easy comparison by readers.

 There are 7 people working in payroll, with a total of 22 working in the overall function. L&D, recruitment and reward employ 3, 4 and 6 people respectively.

numbers (large)

When discussing large numbers in text, it is acceptable to use the following as long as you are consistent throughout the document.

- ✓ k or thousand for 1,000
- ✓ m or million for 1,000,000
- ✓ bn or billion for 1,000,000,000

M

The Roman numeral *M* is often used in financial descriptions to indicate one thousand, and *MM* is used to indicate one million (i.e. a thousand thousand). It tends to be used for larger numbers.

- ✓ £60,000 might appear as £60M.
- ✓ £60,000,000 might appear as £60MM.

Ensure that you use the upper and lower case m/M correctly or if in doubt, use another format. In general, avoid this format as it may cause confusion.

'n'th numbers

Spell out words for 'first', 'second' and so on up to and including 'tenth'; use numbers and superscript 'st'/ 'nd'/ 'rd'/ 'th' for larger ordinal numbers.

- ✓ Manufacturing will be the first division to go live with the new payroll system.
- ✗ This is the 1st time this problem has arisen.

Avoid starting a sentence with a numeral.

- ✗ 2 of the computers are broken.

Do not use slang expressions for numbers in formal writing.

- ✗ We estimate the work will cost around five grand.

Use a combination of figures and words for very large round numbers (such as multiple millions/billions etc.), or abbreviate it to 'm', 'bn' etc.

 The population of the earth is now 7 billion people.

 The budget came in at just under £2m.

numbers between x and y

When using 'between', use a hyphen and include a clearly defined range.

 Between 15-20.

✗ Between 15 to 20.

✗ The total cost of this project is £100–200,000. (The price could start at £100 or £100,000.)

numbers (European format)

Many countries use a full stop (period) to denote a decimal mark including Australia, Canada (when using English), Ireland, Malaysia, Mexico, New Zealand, China, United Kingdom and the United States.

i.e. 1,234,567.89

Continental Europe (plus France, Germany, Greece, Italy, Netherlands, Norway, Poland, Portugal, Romania, Spain, Switzerland, Sweden and French Canada), use the comma or an apostrophe sign to split decimals. This leads to a range of formats:

1234567,89
1.234.567,89
1'234'567.89

O

obviously

Like *basically*, *obviously* is mostly unnecessary and often condescending. If something is obvious, why mention it? But if you do state the obvious, don't insult your readers by using this term.

Avoid *obviously*.

onboarding

While it has its roots in nautical terminology, the term is often used by Human Resources functions to describe the process of bringing new employees into the organisation - figuratively getting them 'on board' the metaphorical corporate ship.

Current convention suggests it is a single word and should not be hyphenated. It should NOT be capitalised unless it refers to a specific module in an HR system.

 We will review our onboarding processes.

 We will review our on boarding processes.

 We will implement the Onboarding module.

one another, each other

see *each other, one another*

ongoing

This word is overstated and bureaucratic. Omit it, or use *continuing, current, developing, under way* or *active*.

past, passed

The word *passed* is the past tense of the verb to *pass*.

✓ She passed the report to me for review.

The word *past* has several meanings, usually related to a time before the present or to indicate movement from one side of a reference point to the other side.

✓ In past years, labour turnover has been high.

See also *homophones*.

percent, per cent

In the UK, per cent is standard, although the US single word percent is commonly used and is becoming standard.

percentages

Always use figures for percentages, measurements and currency, except at the start of a sentence. Use commas to punctuate large numbers.

✓ Only 10% of employees are paid weekly.

✗ 20% of people disagreed with the outcome.

phone numbers (UK)

Use spacing between parts of numbers (international code, area code, phone number) to make it easier to read. Include the full area code (e.g. 01234).

✓ To contact us, ring Bill on 01234 232425

Include the international code for international numbers:

✓ To contact us, ring Bill on +44 1234 232425

Mobile (cellphone) numbers follow the same format as above:

✓ To contact us, ring Bill on 07777 778899

✓ To contact us, ring Bill on +44 7777 778899

For local/internal offices, give extension numbers and include the number to dial from outside the company in brackets.

✓ To contact us, ring Bill on (2)78899

plurals

See *singular, plural*

practice, practise

In UK English, *practice* is a noun and *practise* is a verb:

✓ I am a member of the consultancy practice.

✗ I am a member of the consultancy practise.

✓ I must practise the piano daily.

If you follow US convention, you don't need to worry about this as you can use *practice* for both noun and verb.

pro rata

Pro rata means in proportion. Because it's a Latin phrase, purists argue that you shouldn't tinker with the spelling and should adjust the sentence to retain the original spelling. If you must use derivatives, the past tense should be *pro rated*, not *pro ratad* or worse still, *pro rata'd*. I dislike '*pro ration*' mainly because when spoken it's often pronounced as *pro rash-un* rather than *pro ray-shun*, but that's a personal view.

Or more simply, just say in proportion (to).

preposition

A preposition is a word which shows the relationship to another word in the sentence. Most of the time, a preposition comes before a noun or a pronoun.

Examples are:

above, against, among, around, before, behind, below, beneath, beside, between, beyond, inside, near, toward, through, under, until, up, upon, with and within.

Try to avoid ending a sentence with a preposition. Although it's not really a rule, many people think it is, so to prevent annoying your readers, avoid it.

principle, principal

A *principle* is an idea or guiding argument, either moral or logical:

 A key design principle is that human intervention is kept to a minimum.

*Principal r*efers to the main or most senior:

 I am a principal consultant.

See also *homophones*.

question mark

See full stop, exclamation marks and question mark.

quotation marks

Like brackets in mathematics, quotation marks should be used in pairs. Use double quotes at the start and end of a quoted section.

☑ When interviewed, the finance director said "I entirely agree".

If using a quote within a quote, use single quotes and ensure the same number of single and double quotes on either side.

☑ John said "Bob told me 'never do that again'".

American and British English differ on the placement of full stops (periods) at the end of quotes. American English puts the punctuation before the final "; British English puts punctuation after the ".

☑ "I don't care," she said, "what you think about it." (American)

☑ "I don't care," she said, "what you think about it". (British)

quotes

Copying quotes from academic journals or magazine articles without any form of attribution is plagiarism and legally risky. Regardless of legal issues, it is good practice to say where a quote came from so the reader can refer to the original source (see *references*).

references

When citing quotations from text, always provide a reference. This allows readers to find it themselves. A good format for this is The Harvard referencing style.

 In his 1998 Harvard Business Review paper, Ulrich aks: "Should we do away with HR?" (p.124)

In the references section, include a full citation:

Ulrich, D. (1998) A new mandate for Human Resources. *Harvard Business Review,* January-February, 76 (1), pp. 124-134

regard to, regards to

Several versions of this phrase are in common use, for example, with regard(s) to, in regard(s) of, in regard(s) with.

The general consensus is that *with regard to* is the more accurate, but where possible, you should preferably use a simpler word such as *concerning, about, regarding* or *in relation to*.

regardless, irregardless

There is no such word as *irregardless.*

remuneration, renumeration

Remuneration refers to compensation, reward or a benefits package.

There is no such word as *renumeration* (although it could possibly refer to something that has been re-numbered).

seasons

Seasons do not require the use of capitals:

 When writing for a global audience, remember that summer is different in the Northern and Southern Hemispheres.

See also *holidays*.

semicolon

Like a comma, a semicolon acts like a pause for breath, but it is a slightly longer pause than a comma. Use a semicolon to link two related parts of a sentence, neither of which depends logically on the other and each of which could stand alone as a grammatically complete sentence.

Grammatically, it has the effect of saying "here's something else to think about".

 The best job is the one you enjoy; the worst job is the one you hate.

Use semicolons in place of commas in a complicated list or sentence if it will improve clarity, particularly if there are already commas inside list items. A semicolon should be followed by a single space.

shall

See *will,shall*.

should've/should have/should of

"Should've" is a contraction of "should have" and should not be used in formal writing.

"Should of" is not just lazy - it's totally wrong. It is unacceptable in written and spoken form. See "*could of*"

singular, plural

You can use both the singular and plural forms of verbs that refer to a group. Use the singular when referring to the group as a whole unit and the plural form when the focus is on the group as a collection of individuals.

☑ The board was elected in March.

☑ The board are at each other's throats.

Certain words, including acoustics, ballistics, dynamics, economics, kinetics, mathematics, mechanics, physics and politics are singular.

See also *company names, group*.

sit/sat/sitting

Only objects can be sat down (i.e. placed) somewhere, although people can sit themselves down.

☑ I sat down at the back.

☑ He was sitting near the front.

☒ I was sat on the bus (unless someone picks you up and puts you there).

slang

Readers may not be native British English speakers, so avoid references to nationally known events or people ("he was a bit Del boy") or rhyming slang ("it's all gone Pete Tong").

See also *metaphors*.

slash

\ is a backslash and is not used in written English, only in computing. Unless you're writing about computers or including a URL, don't use a backslash.

/ is a forward slash. A slash can show a line break in a poem, song, or play, usually if several short lines are being written together on one long line.

In business, slashes can also be used to denote a form of abbreviation, although these shouldn't be used in formal writing. In this case, there should be no space after the slash.

☑ w/o = without.

☑ c/o = care of (used when posting a letter or parcel).

A slash can also be used informally to denote a choice between two words.

☑ If/when you are ready, please forward the document to me

smilies and emoticons
Do not use emoticons or any other form of text speak in formal business writing (☺, ☻, LOL, IMHO etc.) unless you are directly quoting someone else's use of them to illustrate a point.

spelled, spelt
Spelt is more common in British English, and *spelled* in American English. The use of *spelt* is considered a spelling error by many Americans, but both are acceptable in the UK.

See also *learned*, *learnt*

split infinitives
Once considered to be practically a criminal offence, splitting infinitives is grammatically correct and may even be useful if it helps strengthen the meaning of a sentence.

☑ It's important to carefully consider the impact of this change.

Avoid awkward sentence constructions that split the infinitive form of a verb, as in this sentence:

 Try to not awkwardly or incorrectly split infinitives.

Unfortunately, split infinitives can distract some readers who think they're being used incorrectly, so it's better to recast the sentence to avoid them.

stationery, stationary

Stationery refers to envelopes, stamps, pens etc.

Tip: 'e' stands for envelope so use the -ery form when spelling stationery.

 The pens are in the stationery cupboard.

Stationary refers to standing still, not moving.

 The car was stationary.

See also *homophones.*

take, bring

See *bring, take*

the

Omitting *"the"* is acceptable in text and emails messages but not in a formal business document such as a report. It breaks the flow of a sentence, is lazy and only benefits the writer. Reconstruct the sentence to avoid it:

   The full report will be sent as soon as possible.

   Full report will be sent as soon as possible.

times

Use either the 12 or 24-hour clock. The 12-hour clock uses a full stop (period) between the hour and minute; the 24-hour clock uses a colon.

   The meeting starts at 11.30am and ends at 1pm.

   The meeting starts at 11:30 and ends at 13:00.

Do not mix formats in the same text.

   The meeting starts at 11.30am and ends at 13:00.

Use 'noon' or 'midnight' instead of '12 noon', '12 midnight' or 12pm

   The closing date for applications is noon on 12 July.

Do not use 'am' or 'pm' with 24-hour times

❌ The meeting starts at 16:00pm.

When using the 12-hour clock, don't use additional '.00' for times on the hour, and close up space between the number and the 'am' or 'pm'.

✅ The meeting starts at 9am.

✅ The meeting starts at 11.30am and ends at 1pm.

❌ The meeting starts at 9.00am.

❌ The meeting starts at 9 am.

time periods

See *dates*

them, those

Using *them* instead of *those* can make you sound uneducated - it's often used to parody uneducated speech as in (adopt redneck drawl) "I'm going to shoot them pesky rabbits".

Those can act as either a pronoun or an adjective:

✅ Please send me those reports. (*Those* is used to describe which reports.)

✅ Those are amazing statistics! (*Those* is used as a simple pronoun acting as the subject of the sentence.)

Them is not a replacement for *those* and never comes before a noun:

❌ Please send me them reports.

❌ Thank you for them emails.

their, they're, there

Their refers to belonging to a group.

☑ It will be done at their own risk.

They're is a contraction of 'they are'.

☑ They're planning a major project.

There refers to a place:

☑ I will see you there at 4pm.

See also *homophones*.

there is, there are, there's, there was, there were

Avoid beginning sentences with these often unnecessary, wordy phrases. Try rewriting the sentence.

☒ There are two payrolls that run every month.

☑ Two payrolls run every month.

There's is a contraction for *there is and* it refers to a single noun. Do not use it with plural nouns.

☒ There's several payrolls running.

therefor, therefore

Therefor is only used by legal people, meaning "for that, for it".
Use *therefore*, or better yet, simplify and use *so, then, thus* instead.

though, although

Although and *though* are used to join parts of a sentence and are interchangeable.

Although is generally considered more formal than *though*.

Though can also mean 'however' or 'nevertheless'. Avoid starting a sentence with *though*.

toward, towards

Toward or *towards* means 'in the direction of'. Toward is more common in American English and towards tends to be used in British English.

U

until such time as; up until
Wordy. Replace with *until*.

upon, on
Opinion is divided on this but the general view is that '*upon*' is antiquated and overly formal. It also alludes to fairy tales ("once upon a time...").

 It depends upon your decision.

Avoid using it to mean 'after':

 Upon receiving your proposal, we will respond.

 When we receive your proposal, we will respond.

URLs
Omit http:// unless the URL does not begin with www and omit any trailing slash at the end of the URL (/), unless the URL does not work without it – check before you omit.

usage, use
The usage of *usage* is mostly incorrect.

Usage means how something is used in terms of custom, habit, tradition or convention, for example, a word, phrase or practice. It can also refer to consumption of water, electricity, gas or other utilities.

In most cases, *use* is the preferred word as a noun and verb, so simplify where possible.

If you must use *usage*, *usage* is the American spelling, although *useage* is sometimes the British English spelling.

☑ This is the correct usage of this word.

☑ The use of this methodology is our preferred approach.

☒ We prefer the usage of this methodology.

utilise, utilisation

Utilise means "putting something to practical, effective use", but *use* is usually less pretentious and formal. Simplify.

☑ We will use PowerPoint for our business presentations.

☒ We will utilise PowerPoint for our business presentations.

verbs

The correct use of verbs could fill its own book. The rules of the English language mean that is very complex to learn all the rules and you must learn the correct way to use every verb in every tense.

A common error is the incorrect use of the PAST PARTICIPLE, which indicates past or completed action or time. It is usually formed by adding *'ed'* to the end of a verb, but there are also many irregular forms which are sometimes confused with the PAST TENSE. Common errors are:

   I have written a song; I have taken a picture, I have run here.

   I have wrote a song; I have took a picture, I have ran here.

Similar errors are commonly made with the following words:

come, came
drank, drunk
did, done
drove, driven
gave, given
run, ran
swam, swum
take, taken

W

was, were

When used in a conditional sense, *was* and *were* can be tricky to get right. "If I were" is appropriate when stating conditions that are contrary to fact.

 If I were a carpenter and you were a lady, would you marry me anyway? (Tim Hardin).

"If I was" is used when stating conditions that are not contrary to fact, or where the truth or falsity of the condition is not certain:

 Was I rude? If I was rude, I'm sorry.

Webex

The general consensus is that the plural of Webex is Webexes.

 We are running a series of Webex's.

 We are running a series of Webexes.

went, gone

See *gone, went*

which, that?

That defines.

Which gives extra information (often in a clause enclosed by commas):

 This is the house that Jack built; but this house, which John built, is falling down.

Note that in these examples, the sentence remains grammatical without "*that*" but not without "*which*".

whether, if

See *if, whether*

while, whilst

Use *while* in preference to *whilst*. *Whilst* is an old English word that sounds increasingly out of date, like 'cometh' and 'amongst'.

Whilst is generally not used outside British English and may confuse international readers; it will sound quaint and possibly pretentious to American readers.

who, whom?

The use of "*whom*" has mostly disappeared from spoken English, and seems to be disappearing from written English. Concern about using the right form can terrify even the most confident users of grammar. Here's how to use it properly:

Who does something, and *whom* has something done to it.

Use *who* when someone takes an action as the subject of a sentence, clause or phrase. Use *whom* when someone is the object:

Tip: Turn the sentence around and add a person in. If the person turns into he/she/they, then "who" is right; if it becomes him/her/them, then it should be "whom".

- ☑ Who wrote the letter? (Did <u>he</u> write the letter = who).
- ☑ Whom do you wish to see? (Do you wish to see him = whom).

If you are not sure, it is much better to use "*who*" than to use "*whom*" incorrectly. Even when it is used correctly, the use of 'whom' can sound pompous, so take great care.

who, which, that

Who in a sentence should only refer to people.

☑ Send the report to Bill, who will then file it.

Which introduces a non-essential clause. It can only refer to things, not people.

☑ Send the report to the Finance Department, which will then file it.

Use *which* NOT *who*, as the Finance Department is not a person. If a person is named, it becomes *who*.

☑ Send the report to Bill in the Finance Department, who will then file it.

That introduces an essential clause, something that provides important information. *That* is often favoured in American English.

☑ This is the report that will change everything.

Just to make things complicated, in the above example, British English would be perfectly happy with the use of *which*.

who's, whose

Who's is a contraction of *who is* or *who has*, not a possessive:

☑ Who's going to make the tea?

For the possessive (belonging), use *whose*.

☑ I do not know whose laptop this is.

will, shall

Shall should only be used when referring to the first person (I or we), although this tends not to be used in American English.

In theory, *will* and *shall* are interchangeable, although *will* is far more common. *Shall* tends to be used to mean an obligation, threat or command and *will* to mean desire or intention.

Indeed, the US Government's Plain Language group advises writers not to use the word *shall* – take care when using *shall* in case its meaning is misinterpreted.

would have/would of

See *could have, should have*.

you, yourself

See my/myself.

Yours faithfully

This is the standard end to a letter where you do not know the name of the person you are writing to, for example, the Accounts Department. The 'faithfully' part does not need to be capitalised.

Yours sincerely

This is the standard end to a letter where you know the name of the person you are writing to, that is, a person named at the start of the letter. The 'sincerely' part does not need to be capitalised.

Z

The possessive form of words ending in "Z" is to add an apostrophe and "s"

 This is Aziz's desk

OK, strictly this should have appeared under apostrophes, but there really aren't any grammatical concepts starting with Z.....

Guidelines for good writing

Plain English is at the heart of any good business document. If you truly understand what your report or document is trying to say, simple language will flow. If, however, you are unsure of your argument, you are likely to use overly complex words and pretentious language to disguise your lack of knowledge. Bad writing often reveals a poor argument.

George Orwell observed that a scrupulous writer will ask the following questions:

- What am I trying to say?
- What words will express it?
- What image or idiom will make it clearer?
- Is my writing fresh enough to have an effect?
- Could I express it in fewer words?
- Have I said anything that is avoidably ugly?

Orwell defined five rules of writing:

1. Never use a long word where a short one will do.
2. If it is possible to cut out a word, always cut it out.
3. Never use the passive word where you can use the active.
4. Never use a foreign phrase, a scientific word or a jargon word if you can think of an everyday English equivalent.
5. Break any of these rules rather than say anything outright barbarous.

Use the language of everyday speech, not that of civil servants, lawyers and bureaucrats. Pomposity and long-windedness tend to obscure meaning, or reveal the lack of it: strip them away in favour of plain words.

clichés

The use of clichés, jargon, buzzwords and management speak is generally detrimental to good writing. Often, certain phrases that form part of normal speech are used without even thinking about them. Overused words and phrases should be avoided in written text as they make the writer sound unimaginative. Among the most irritating phrases in written documents are:

At this moment in time	Going forward
Blue sky thinking	Ballpark figure
Bring it to the table	Move the goalposts
Mission critical	Think outside the box
Pushing the envelope	Win-win situation
Take it to the next level	Client focus

management speak

'Management speak' is a form of cliché, often used to make something seem more impressive than it actually is.

Scott Adams (of Dilbert fame) provides a good example of management speak in a corporate mission statement:

"*to scout profitable growth opportunities in relationships, both internally and externally, in emerging, mission-inclusive markets, and explore new paradigms and then filter and communicate and evangelize the findings.*"

I recommend the website www.bollocksphere.co.uk for good (i.e. terrible) examples of management speak.

proofreading

Before submitting any email, report or document, read it, read it again and if necessary, get someone else to read it for you. Good quality writing, with no errors, allows your work to be taken seriously.

Writing a business report

Structure

There are many different ways to write a good business report, but the basic format is the same whether you are writing a one page report or a PhD thesis. Essentially, it boils down to 'what was the problem, how did you try to solve it, what did you find, what happens next?'

Try to break up the report into meaningful sections and ensure the layout is pleasing to look at. People are more likely to read a document if it is uncluttered and properly formatted. Long paragraphs - like long sentences - can intimidate readers. To improve readability and appearance, try to limit paragraphs to eight lines containing no more than four or five sentences.

Here's one suggestion for laying out a report:

- **The executive summary** – this should provide a brief synopsis of the key points, including the problem being addressed, how it was approached, the conclusion and recommendations. The target audience for this section is anyone with an interest in the issues who may not read the full report. A typical executive summary should be no more than 5% of the overall length of the report. If the report contains fewer than 2,000 words, an executive summary may get in the way. An executive summary should contain no new information – otherwise it's not a summary!

- **Background/overview** – what is the purpose of the document, what is the business problem it seeks to address, who was it written for, what does it hope to achieve? When was it carried out and at the time were there any special factors to be taken into account?

- **Key issues** – expand on the key business issues that are being investigated, how did they arise, why are they important now?

- **Approach** – how was the work carried out and where? If it was through interviews, make sure you include a list of those interviewed and their roles.

- **Findings** – what did you find out during the research or investigation? What evidence did you find to support your conclusions?

- **Recommendations** – consider what options are available and the relative merits of each. Provide data as necessary but do not let the data stop the flow of the report. Explain what should happen next and why.

- **Appendices** – this is useful way of gathering a range of charts, tables and details without cluttering the main body of the document. Make sure they are fully cross-referenced with the main body of the document.

- **References** – provide references for any academic, online or press based source material, using a standard referencing format.

Writing style
As a general rule, always write in the active voice. The active voice is simpler, more direct and more forceful than the passive voice and flows better. In some contexts, passive writing can sound pompous and condescending. Avoid shifts between active and passive within a sentence.

 The payroll manager checked the data.

 The data was checked by the payroll manager.

Diagrams
When inserting a diagram, always explain what the diagram means and why it is relevant. Never insert a diagram without explaining what it is for and the point it supports. Label the diagram (for example, table 1, figure 1) and refer to it in the text.

Microsoft Word can create a separate table of contents for tables and figures if you have a large report.

email etiquette

Unlike text messages or social media, which involve short, snappy messages, an email is the equivalent to a traditional business letter or memorandum and should be handled carefully, not least because of the legal implications where customers or suppliers are concerned.

The following are my top twenty email rules:

1. Use a meaningful subject in the subject field (not something generic like 'order' or 'job'.
2. Use the cc: field sparingly – if someone is not in the main recipient list, assume they will take no action in response to your email.
3. Check the recipient's address – many email programs have predictive text for addresses and you may accidentally send it to the wrong person. At best it will be inconvenient, at worst commercially catastrophic.
4. Do not write in CAPITALS.
5. Add disclaimers to your emails – apply whatever standard legal requirements your company requires.
6. Put your contact details at the bottom of the email, such as your phone number. These can be set up as a standard signature.
7. Be concise and to the point.
8. Avoid long sentences.
9. Use proper spelling, grammar and punctuation.
10. Do not attach unnecessary files and do not attach multiple files.
11. Do not force recipients to read an attachment in order to understand your point – summarise and refer to attachments as you would an appendix in a document.
12. Read the email before you send it (always!).
13. Do not overuse Reply to All, especially if responding to a group email, it just creates more junk.

14. Do not request delivery and read receipts (it's a little rude and suggests the recipient might deny receiving it).
15. Do not ask to recall a message.
16. Do not copy or forward a message or attachment without permission.
17. Do not use email to discuss confidential information.
18. Do not forward chain letters, hoaxes, libelous, defamatory, offensive, racist or obscene remarks or reply to spam.
19. Do not write an angry or emotional email (or if you must, walk away from it for a couple of hours then review).
20. Ask whether an email is the most appropriate format – long, rambling emails may not get read or will slip down someone's inbox.

Mangled phrases

The following phrases are often mangled, together with the correct versions:

Mangled	Correct
All of the sudden	All of a sudden
Baited breath	Bated breath
Beckon call	Beck and call
By in large	By and large
Case and point	Case in point
Damp squid	Damp squib
Doggy dog world	Dog eat dog world
Fall by the waste side	Fall by the wayside
Fall fowl of…	Fall foul of…
Four warned is four armed	Fore warned is fore armed
For all intensive purposes	For all intents and purposes
In sink	In sync
Mute point	Moot point
One foul swoop	One fell swoop
One in the same	One and the same
On tender hooks	On tenterhooks
Slight of hand	Sleight of hand
Statue of limitations	Statute of limitations
Suppose to	Supposed to
Swinging roundabouts	Swings and roundabouts
To the tenth degree	To the nth degree
Tow the line	Toe the line
You have another thing coming	You have another think coming
Wreck havoc	Wreak havoc

References

Adams, S. (2007), The Dilbert Principle

Brians, P. (2013), Common Errors in English Usage, third edition, William, James & Company: Sherwood, Oregon

The Economist Style Guide (2012), Profile Books

The Elements of Style (1979), Strunk, W., White, E.B., New York: Longman

Truss, L. Eats, Shoots and Leaves (2003), Profile Books, London

Useful Websites

www.Bollocksphere.co.uk
http://garbl.home.comcast.net
www.Grammarly.com
www.grammar-monster.com
www.theguardian.com/guardian-observer-style-guide-a
www.MyEnglishGrammar.com
http://thegrammarexchange.infopop.cc/eve
www.Oxford dictionaries.com

www.ingramcontent.com/pod-product-compliance
Lightning Source LLC
Chambersburg PA
CBHW072229170526
45158CB00002BA/820